AMERICAN HUMANE

Protecting Children & Animals Since 1877

Top 10 Fish for Kids

Dana Meachen Rau

Enslow Elementary

an imprint of

 Enslow Publishers, Inc.
40 Industrial Road
Box 398
Berkeley Heights, NJ 07922
USA

http://www.enslow.com

AMERICAN HUMANE

Protecting Children & Animals Since 1877

Founded in 1877, the American Humane Association is the oldest national organization dedicated to protecting both children and animals. Through a network of child and animal protection agencies and individuals, the American Humane Association develops policies, legislation, curricula, and training programs to protect children and animals from abuse, neglect, and exploitation. To learn how you can support the vision of a nation where no child or animal will ever be a victim of willful abuse or neglect, visit www.americanhumane.org, phone (303) 792-9900, or write to the American Humane Association at 63 Inverness Drive East, Englewood, Colorado, 80112-5117.

Enslow Elementary, an imprint of Enslow Publishers, Inc.

Enslow Elementary® is a registered trademark of Enslow Publishers, Inc.

The top 10 fish are approved by the American Humane Association and are listed alphabetically.

Library of Congress Cataloging-in-Publication Data

Rau, Dana Meachen, 1971–
    Top 10 fish for kids / Dana Meachen Rau.
        p. cm. — (Top pets for kids with American Humane)
    Summary: "Provides facts on the top ten fish breeds for kids and how to care for them"—Provided by publisher.
    Includes bibliographical references and index.
    ISBN-13: 978-0-7660-3073-2
    ISBN-10: 0-7660-3073-3
    1. Aquarium fishes—Juvenile literature. I. Title. II. Title: Top ten fish for kids.
    SF457.25.R38 2008
    639.34—dc22

                                    2007032319

Printed in the United States of America

10 9 8 7 6 5 4 3 2 1

To Our Readers:
We have done our best to make sure that all Internet Addresses in this book were active and appropriate when we went to press. However, the author and publisher have no control over and assume no liability for the material available on those Internet sites or on other Web sites they may link to. Any comments or suggestions can be sent by e-mail to comments@enslow.com or to the address on the back cover.

♻ Enslow Publishers, Inc., is committed to printing our books on recycled paper. The paper in every book contains 10% to 30% post-consumer waste (PCW). The cover board on the outside of each book contains 100% PCW. Our goal is to do our part to help young people and the environment too!

Cover Photo: Carol Buchanan/Alamy
Interior Photos: Alamy/Maximilian Weinzierl, pp. 3, 4, 39, 40; Alamy/Juniors Bildarchiv, pp. 8, 14; Alamy/PCPhotoStock, p. 20; Alamy/blickwinkel, pp. 21, 36, 38; Alamy/Jane Gould, p. 26; Alamy/Andre Seale, p. 27; Alamy/David Fleetham, p. 30; Alamy/Martin Harvey, p. 32; Alamy/Peter Arnold, Inc., p. 34; Alamy/Visual&Written SL, pp. 37, 44; Alamy/Arco Images, p. 41; Alamy/vario images GmbH & Co.KG, p. 43; Acclaim Images/Fred Voetsch, p. 2; Acclaim Images/Edward Greenberg, p. 24; Animals Animals–Earth Scenes/M. Gibbs/OSF, pp. 19, 28, 48; Custom Medical Stock Photo/Educational Images Ltd., p. 15; Getty Images/Dave King, p. 23; iStockphoto.com/ActinicBlue, p. 1; iStockphoto.com/Lise Gagne, pp. 5, 7, 9, 17, 42; iStockphoto.com/Krzysztof Rafa, p. 10; iStockphoto.com/Rosica Daskalova, p. 22; iStockphoto.com/Eric Isselée, pp. 25, 31, 33; iStockphoto.com/Sue McDonald, p. 35; iStockphoto.com/Brian Dombrowski, p. 46; Jupiterimages/Hemera Technologies, p. 11; Lucky Oliver/khz, p. 47; Photo Edit/Michael Newman, pp. 13, 16; Photo Researchers, Inc./Tierbild Okapia, p. 6.

Contents

So You Want to Get a Fish?

The underwater world is a fascinating place. There are fish of all shapes, sizes, and colors. You can learn to scuba dive to get a look at these interesting swimmers up close. Or you can watch them right in your home!

If you are thinking of getting a pet fish, make sure it is a family decision.

◀ A home aquarium is a fascinating underwater world. You create it yourself, and fill it with your own fish.

▲

A person who keeps an aquarium is called an aquarist.

Talk together about what kind of pet you would like. Fish are a lot of fun to watch. But that is about all you can do with them. You cannot cuddle or play with a fish like you can with a cat or a dog.

As with any pet, you are responsible for taking care of a fish. You have to make sure it has a good home (tank), gets the right food to eat, and stays healthy.

Do you have time every day to feed your fish? Do you have time every week to clean the tank? Will you be willing to take care of a fish for its whole life? While fish can get sick easily and may only live a few weeks or months, many live for a few years. Others, with the right care, can live even longer. Keeping a home aquarium is a lot of work.

Fish also need a lot of equipment. After you decide what kind of fish you want, you will need to get and set up the equipment. Your first stop will be the pet store or aquarium store.

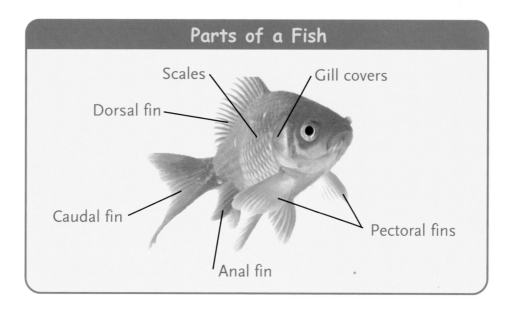

Parts of a Fish

Scales

Gill covers

Dorsal fin

Caudal fin

Pectoral fins

Anal fin

An Aquarium to Call Home

There are two types of fish—freshwater and saltwater. In the wild, freshwater fish live in lakes, ponds, and streams. Saltwater fish live in the ocean. Saltwater tanks are also called marine tanks. It is best to start off keeping and taking care of a freshwater tank. It can be very complicated to set up and take care of a marine tank. Because of this,

◄ A freshwater aquarium holds fish that live in lakes, ponds, and streams in the wild. These include platys, which are popular pet fish.

saltwater fish are recommended only for people with a lot of experience keeping fish.

Tanks and Supplies

Some experts say that you should start with a 25- to 50-gallon tank. Others say a 10-gallon

▲

Live plants make great hiding places for fish in an aquarium. They also help keep the water clean. Like your fish, they need special care.

tank is fine. The biggest tank you can afford (and that you have room for) will be the best choice. It will give your fish more room to swim and less of a chance of getting sick from dirty water.

Your tank will also need a hood with a light. Light will help your fish stay healthy. If you have live plants in your tank, they need light to survive. You will need a heater and a thermometer to check the water temperature. Finally, the tank needs a filter. The filter sucks in water, cleans it, then puts it back into the tank.

You will need gravel and decorations. You can use live plants in the tanks, too. Live plants help keep the water healthy. But they need special care. Ask at the pet store to find out the best type of plant for the fish you are planning to take home. You can also decorate the tank with plastic plants made especially for home aquariums. Other aquarium decorations, such as a treasure chest or castle are fun. These decorations, made especially for fish tanks, give your fish places to hide.

Setting Up the Tank

Now that you have all the equipment, it is time to start setting up. First, make sure you choose a strong and solid stand or piece of furniture to hold your tank. Your tank can weigh a hundred pounds or more when filled with water.

Where should you place the tank? First of all, it will need to be near an electrical outlet, to plug in the filter, light, and heater. It should also be near a water source, because you will need to change the water regularly. Remember, water and electricity can be dangerous together. So you need to find a place where your tank cannot be knocked over. You should not put it in an area where there is a lot of activity. A corner is often a good place.

Be sure to put your fish tank on a sturdy piece of furniture. The tank might weigh a hundred pounds or more when it is filled with water.

▼

Fish do not like changes in water temperature. Do not put the tank near windows where the sun can heat up their water. Also avoid any area near a heating vent, fireplace, or radiator. Instead, try to choose an area for the tank where the water temperature is likely to remain the same all the time.

▲

An aquarium thermometer is important for making sure the water temperature always stays the same.

Fish are also very sensitive to sound. So do not put the tank right near a television or stereo where they might feel a lot of vibration. For the same reason, never bang on the glass to get your fish's attention.

To fill the tank, use water from the faucet that has been tested and adjusted to make sure it is just right for your fish to survive. It may have some things in it that can harm your fish, such as a chemical called chlorine. You should also test the water with something called a pH kit. With this test you can make sure the water is safe for your fish.

Talk to someone at the store where you bought your fish for more information and details about setting up your tank. He or she will know a lot about fish tanks and can probably give you good advice.

▲

It is important to use a pH kit to test the water in your tank. This will tell you that the water is safe for your fish.

Choosing Your Pet Fish

There are so many different types of fish, it can be difficult to decide which kind is right for you. And how many should you get?

The number of fish that can live in your tank depends on the size of the tank. A general rule is one inch of fish per gallon of water, as long as the fish are slim and no more than three or four

There are a lot of things to think about when trying to decide which of the many types of fish to get.

inches long. For example, a 25-gallon tank can be a comfortable home for 25 "inches" of fish. In other words, if your fish are all about two inches long, that means about 12 fish.

It is a good idea to start with just three or four fish. Make sure to pick a kind of fish that can survive in the harsh water conditions of a new tank. These fish will "prepare" the tank for more fish.

When fish "breathe" through their gills, and when they go to the bathroom, their waste contains ammonia. Too much ammonia in the water can kill fish. But luckily, there are types of bacteria that need ammonia to live. They change the ammonia to a less harmful substance so the water is safe for the fish.

This process takes a few weeks. Then you can have the water tested to be sure that there are enough bacteria now to handle the waste of more fish.

When you go to pick out your fish, you will notice that some aquarium fish are very expensive, while others cost less. But price is not the only thing to think about.

If you want to have a community tank, where there will be more than one fish, you have to find fish that will get along with each other. Some fish are very aggressive.

For a community tank, it is very important to choose fish that can live together peacefully.

▲

Each type of fish has its own needs. Some prefer to live in a tank by themselves.

They might eat all of the food so that more timid fish cannot get to their meal. Some fish eat smaller fish. Some like to be in a school, or group of fish. Some fish lay eggs. Some fish are livebearers, which means they give birth to live young. A male and female fish of the same kind may mate and give you many more baby fish.

Look for a healthy fish. Check that it has clear eyes and that it does not have any spots or sores on its body. It should be active and alert. If any fish in the tank looks sick, buy from a different tank. Diseases spread easily in water.

Once you have chosen your fish and brought it home, float the bag on the top of the tank for about 15 minutes. This will help the fish get used to the temperature of the water. Then add some water from the tank to the fish's bag a few times to help it get used to the new water. After about half an hour, move your fish from the bag into the tank with a soft net.

▲

Fish need several minutes to get used to the temperature of the water in a new tank.

Angelfish are originally from the central Amazon River in South America.

Appearance

- Come in many colors, such as silver, black, and gold
- Very long fins
- Flat, triangle-shaped body
- Grow to about 5 inches in length

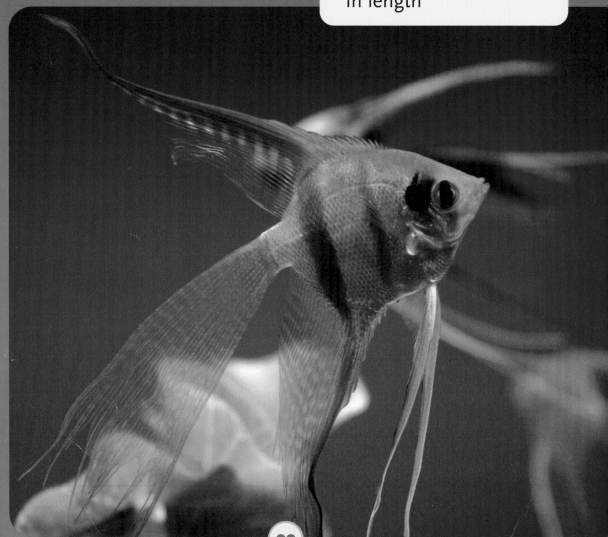

Angelfish

When a female and male angelfish get together, they stay together for life. They mate only with each other. In the wild, angelfish live in the central Amazon River in South America.

Special Needs

Angelfish need a warm freshwater tank with water temperature between 72° and 82° F. They need a deep tank because of their body shape, as well as places to hide. They will be healthiest if you feed them a mixture of flake, frozen, and live food.

General Behavior

Angelfish:

1. are peaceful fish, and can be good in a community tank if they were raised in it. Sometimes older angelfish and those that are mating can be aggressive.
2. may get bothered by fish that like to nip long fins.
3. might eat smaller fish, such as neon tetras.

◀ Angelfish like to hide. Plenty of aquarium plants will give them great hiding places.

Bettas are sometimes called Siamese fighting fish.

Appearance

- Come in many colors, such as red, blue, green, black, and yellow
- Long, flowing fins. Females have shorter fins than males.
- Grow to about 2.5 inches in length

Betta
(Siamese Fighting Fish)

Bettas are sometimes called Siamese fighting fish. They are originally from Thailand (once called Siam) and other areas of Southern Asia.

Special Needs

Bettas need a freshwater tank with the water at a temperature between 75° and 86° F. They may jump out of the water, so you must cover the tank. Use something that still lets air through, such as a screen.

General Behavior

Bettas:

1. are peaceful unless two males are put in a tank together. Males will fight each other until one dies. Some tanks have special barriers, or boxes that hang off the side to keep males separate.

2. should not be kept in community tanks, because they will eat smaller fish and may get bothered by fish that like to nip long fins.

3. do best by themselves.

◀ Unlike other fish, bettas do not have gills. They breathe air from the water's surface.

Blue-green chromis get along with most other fish.

Appearance

- Greenish coloring over the whole body
- Short, pointed fins, and a forked tail fin
- Grow to about 2 inches in length

Blue-Green Chromis

Blue-green chromis are a type of damselfish. Most damselfish are aggressive and like to be alone. Blue-green chromis, however, swim in schools and get along with other fish. They are from coral reefs in the Indian Ocean and Western Pacific. They are saltwater fish. You may need the help of an adult to care for them properly.

Special Needs

Blue-green chromis need a

General Behavior

Blue-green chromis:

1. are peaceful and shy.
2. are good for community tanks because they get along with most other fish.
3. like to swim in a school, so get at least four of them for your tank.

marine (saltwater) tank with water temperature between 75° and 82° F. Be on the lookout for blue-green chromis that spend their time hiding. They may feel threatened by other fish in the tank. Having a small school of blue-green chromis can prevent that, since they feel safer in a group.

◀ **Blue-green chromis are saltwater fish that swim in a school, or group.**

Brazilian sea horses spend time holding onto grass with their curly tails.

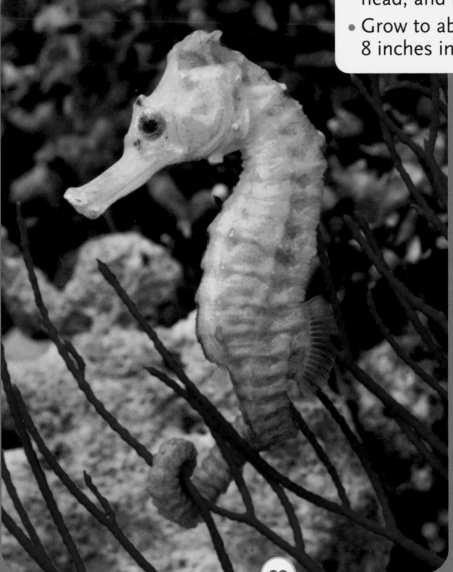

Appearance

- Come in black, brown, and yellow. Some have bands and spots of color.
- Curly tail, horse-shaped head, and long snout
- Grow to about 4 to 8 inches in length

Brazilian Sea Horse

Brazilian sea horses swim vertically (up and down), not horizontally (side-to-side) like other fish. They are originally from the Western Caribbean. Many colorful examples were found in the waters off Brazil, which is how they got their name. They are saltwater fish. You may need the help of an adult to care for them properly.

General Behavior

Brazilian sea horses:

1. are peaceful fish.
2. swim slowly.
3. live best as a male and female pair or with other Brazilian sea horses.
4. spend time holding onto grass with their curly tails.
5. are carnivores (meat eaters), so they like to eat live and frozen saltwater shrimp.

Special Needs

Brazilian sea horses need a marine tank with water temperature between 72° and 82° F. The tank should be at least 29 to 55 gallons. It should have lots of plants that they can grasp with their tails. Brazilian sea horses cannot be in a tank with fast-moving water because they are not strong swimmers.

◄ Brazilian sea horses swim slowly. They should not share a tank with faster fish that will eat up all the food.

Clownfish are
saltwater fish.

Appearance

- Yellow-orange body with three bands of white that have thin black bands
- Double fins
- Grow to about 2.75 inches in length

Clownfish

General Behavior

Clownfish:

1. are peaceful fish. However, a male clownfish will chase fish away from its territory, especially other male clownfish.
2. live best alone or as a male and female pair.
3. are aggressive eaters.

Clownfish are also called anemone (a-NEM-a-nee) fish. This is because in the wild they live among the tentacles (arms) of anemone. Anemone are sea animals related to corals and jellyfish.

Clownfish are originally from the coral reefs of the Indian Ocean and Western Pacific. They are saltwater fish. You may need the help of an adult to care for them properly.

Special Needs

Clownfish need a marine tank with water temperature between 75° and 82° F. They are used to living among anemone in the wild, so their tank will need anemone or a cave-like place for the clownfish to hide.

◀ The waving tentacles of an anemone are home to these two clownfish in the wild.

31

Goldfish were one of the first fish to be kept and bred as pets.

Goldfish

Goldfish are a favorite first fish for many people because they are so easy to take care of. Goldfish are originally from Asia and parts of Eastern Europe. They were one of the first fish to be kept and bred as pets.

General Behavior

Goldfish:

1. are peaceful fish.
2. are good for community tanks with other fish that prefer cold water, but live best with other goldfish.

Special Needs

Goldfish need a cold, freshwater tank with water temperature between 64° to 70° F, so they do not do well with tropical freshwater fish that need warmer water. Goldfish grow fast and create a lot of waste, so be sure the tank is big enough. Never put them in a fishbowl, which does not have enough room for the fish to swim, and will not let them get enough oxygen. Goldfish need a good filter that cleans the water and puts in a lot of air. They also need places to hide.

◄ Goldfish will eat as much food as you give them, so be careful not to overfeed them.

Guppies are good for community tanks.

Appearance

- Come in red, green, black, and many other colors and combinations
- Males are colorful, while females are a dull gray
- Long, flowing fins in different shapes, such as rounded, swordtail, and fantail. Females have much smaller fins than males.
- Grow to about 1.25 inches in length

Guppy

Have you ever heard anyone described as a "small fry"? "Fry" is the term for baby fish. You will soon have your own crowd of small fry if you decide to put male and female guppies in your tank! In the wild, these fish live in the waters of the Caribbean Islands, upper South America, and Central America.

General Behavior

Guppies:
1. are peaceful fish.
2. are good fish to have in community tanks.
3. may get bothered by fish that nip at long fins. They also nip at the long fins of other fish.
4. could be eaten if put in a tank with larger fish.
5. mate easily.

Special Needs

Guppies need a freshwater tank with water temperature between 72° and 82° F. Guppies like their water a little salty, so you can add about 1 teaspoon of aquarium salt per gallon of water (be sure never to use regular table salt!).

◄ Guppies give birth to live fry. Plants make a good hiding place for the fry so they are not eaten by other fish.

Mollies have a variety of fin shapes.

- Can be green, black, silver, or gold
- A variety of fin types, such as sailfin and lyre tail. The common molly, also known as the short finned molly, has small fins.

Molly

In a group of mollies, one fish usually becomes dominant over the others. This is one reason that mollies are fun to watch. These fish are originally from the southern United States, South America, and Central America.

General Behavior

Mollies:
1. do very well in community tanks.
2. may nip at slower fish.

Special Needs

Mollies need a freshwater tank with water temperature between 72° and 82° F. They especially like plenty of plants for hiding. Mollies also like their water to be a little salty, so you can add about 1 teaspoon of aquarium salt per gallon of water.

◄ Mollies are live-bearing fish, which means they give birth to live young.

Neon tetras like to swim in a school.

Appearance

- Slim bodies with a blue stripe from head to tail, silver on top, and red on the bottom
- Very pointed fins and a forked caudal fin
- Grow to about 1 inch in length

Neon Tetra

A neon tetra's colors are brightest when it is active during the day. The colors are duller when the fish is resting at night. Neon tetras are originally from the rivers of South America.

Special Needs

Neon tetras need a warm freshwater tank with water temperature between 72° and 82° F. They need lots of space to swim, since they are a schooling fish. But they also like lots of hiding places. Neon tetras cannot be in a tank with large fish, because they will be eaten. They are best with fish of their own size.

General Behavior

Neon tetras:
1. are shy.
2. are good fish to have in community tanks.
3. like to swim in a school, so you should get five or more.

◄ Tiny neon tetras make a colorful display as they swim around in a large school.

Platys are active, and need room to swim around.

Appearance

- Come in many colors, such as red, blue, black, gold, and even rainbow. Females can be a little duller.
- Rounded caudal fin, and a large dorsal fin
- Grow to about 1.5 inches in length

Platy

Platys are sometimes called moonfish because of a crescent shape at the base of their tails, especially in gold ones. These fish are originally from the Atlantic coastal waters of Mexico, Guatemala, and Honduras in Central America.

General Behavior

Platys:

1. are peaceful fish.
2. are good fish to have in community tanks.
3. can be active and might bother slower moving fish, such as angelfish.
4. mate easily, so a male and female in the same tank will make many fry.

Special Needs

Platys need a freshwater tank with water temperature between 72° and 82° F. They like their water to be a little salty, so you can add about 1 teaspoon of aquarium salt per gallon of water.

◄ Platys like a well-lit tank with plants to hide in, and plenty of room to swim around.

Keeping Your Fish Healthy

One of the most important things you will need to do to keep your fish healthy is to change the water in the tank every one to two weeks to keep it clean. When you add new water, be sure it is treated to adjust its pH or chlorine level. Also make sure it is about the same temperature as the water in the tank. Every four to six weeks, you will also need to clean or change the filter.

▲

It is important to vacuum the gravel in your tank every so often. Uneaten food can settle in the gravel and decay, making the water dirty.

Feeding

You will need to feed your fish twice a day, morning and night. Be very careful not to overfeed them. You should feed your fish only as much as they can eat in three to five minutes. The type of food will depend on your fish.

Health Care

After many weeks of watching your fish, you will know how each one behaves. You will

Watch your fish every day and get to know their normal behavior. This will help you recognize if one of them becomes ill.

be able to tell when any of your fish are sick, because it will look or act different than usual.

Notice the way your fish swims. Is it darting around the tank, or is it moving slowly? Is it at the surface, or is it lying on the bottom of the tank? Look at your fish's body. Are its eyes cloudy or fins split? Has it changed color or developed spots? This might mean your fish is sick.

Most illnesses are caused by the water in the tank. You must regularly check the water with a test kit. Also be sure to check that the filter is working correctly. If needed, clean the tank and bring in some new, clean water.

If a fish dies, remove it from the tank with a net as soon as possible so it will not make the other fish sick.

Do not flush a dead fish down the toilet. It will get into waterways and might spread its illness to other fish in the wild. You can bury your fish outdoors in the ground. Or you can place it in a bag and put it in the trash.

Unlike other pets, fish do not need to be petted, brushed, or taken on walks. They do not need toys to play with or constant attention from you. But they do rely on you to survive. It is your job as their owner to make their tank a place where they can live a happy and healthy life.

Glossary

anemone—An animal with long arm-like tentacles that gives clownfish a place to hide.

chlorine—A chemical in water that can be dangerous to fish.

community tank—A tank with many types of fish living together.

filter—Part of a tank that sucks in water, cleans it, then puts it back into the tank.

fry—Baby fish.

gills—Parts of a fish's body that allow it to breathe under water.

live-bearer—Fish that gives birth to live young instead of laying eggs.

marine tank—A saltwater tank.

pH kit—A kit that tests the water in a fish tank. It will tell you if the water is safe for fish.

school—A group of fish of the same kind.

territory—Area an animal lives in that it tries to protect.

Further Reading

Lundblad, Kristina, and Bobbie Kalman. *Animals Called Fish*. New York: Crabtree Publishing Company, 2005.

MacAulay, Kelley, and Bobbie Kalman. *Goldfish*. New York: Crabtree Publishing Company, 2005.

Richardson, Adele. *Caring For Your Fish*. Mankato, Minn.: Capstone Press, 2007.

Silverstein, Virginia, Alvin Silverstein, and Laura Silverstein Nunn. *Fabulous Fish*. Brookfield, Conn.: Twenty-First Century Books, 2003.

Internet Addresses

American Humane Association
www.americanhumane.org

ASPCA Animaland
www.animaland.org

Index